YOU

1966

THIS

MILESTONES, MEMORIES,
TRIVIA AND FACTS, NEWS EVENTS,
PROMINENT PERSONALITIES &
SPORTS HIGHLIGHTS OF THE YEAR

TO : _____

FROM : _____

MESSAGE : _____

_____

*selected and researched
by
mary a. pradt*

WARNER ⓦ TREASURES™

PUBLISHED BY WARNER BOOKS

A TIME WARNER COMPANY

Warner Books, Inc.
1271 Avenue of the Americas
New York, New York 10020

Warner Treasures is a
trademark of Warner Books, Inc.

Ⓦ A Time Warner Company

DESIGN:
CAROL BOKUNIEWICZ DESIGN
PRINTED IN SINGAPORE
FIRST PRINTING : MAY 1995
10 9 8 7 6 5 4 3 2 1
ISBN : 0-446-91043-0

Parades and protests grew in size, variety, frequency, and intensity. On March 31 more than 20,000 demonstrated in NY; counter-demonstrators threw eggs. Monthly draft calls grew to ten times the 1965 average. In April, for the first time, American combat deaths

Opposition to the Vietnam War grew.

exceeded South Vietnamese. By the end of May, with American deaths rising, a crowd of 8,000 gathered in Washington and declared the war "unwinnable." Student protests gathered speed and stridency. Demonstrators at Dow Chemical headquarters compared the manufacture of napalm with Nazi atrocities. On December 26, 1966, the Defense Department admitted to accidental deaths of civilians during attacks on North Vietnamese/Viet Cong military targets.

THE FIRST ARTIFICIAL HEART PUMP WAS IMPLANTED IN A HUMAN PATIENT; LEAD SURGEON WAS MICHAEL DEBAKEY IN HOUSTON.

RACE LOOMED LARGE AS A NATIONAL CONCERN. James Meredith, who had integrated "Ole Miss" in 1962, was shot in the back June 6. **Dr. Martin Luther King, Jr.,** and 208 others were teargassed while marching in Mississippi. Racial riots occurred in a "long hot summer" in Chicago, New York, and Cleveland.

AMERICAN CATHOLICS were no longer required to abstain from meat on Fridays — except during Lent — because of a decision by the Vatican.

THE BLACK PANTHER

party was founded in Oakland, CA.

ON AUGUST 1, 1966, A FORMER ALTAR BOY, EAGLE SCOUT, AND HONORS STUDENT, CHARLES WHITMAN, 25, CLIMBED TO THE TOP OF A TOWER AT THE UNIVERSITY OF TEXAS IN AUSTIN AND SHOT 12 PEOPLE DEAD, LEAVING 33 OTHERS WOUNDED. WHITMAN WAS KILLED BY A POLICE OFFICER DURING THE SIEGE.

newsreel

THE NATIONAL ORGANIZATION FOR WOMEN WAS FOUNDED.

edward brooke,

the former Massachusetts attorney general, became the first Black to be elected to the U.S. Senate since Reconstruction. Reconstruction – era Blacks who served in the Senate 85 years earlier had been elected by Mississippi legislators, not by the voters at large.

It was a good year in space. The first Apollo test flight was a success. The last Gemini mission, *Gemini 12*, was, too. Edwin "Buzz" Aldrin and James Lovell landed their craft in the Atlantic in November. Aboard *Gemini 11* in September, astronauts Charles Conrad, Jr., and Richard F. Gordon, Jr., set an altitude record of 851 miles and rendezvoused in space.

"ONE OF OUR H-BOMBS IS MISSING." EMBARRASSINGLY FOR THE U.S., A HYDROGEN BOMB FELL OFF A B-52 BOMBER OFF THE COAST OF SPAIN AND WAS MISSING FOR TWO MONTHS. IT WAS LOCATED BY A MIDGET SUBMARINE ON APRIL 7. THE SPANISH POPULATION HAD BEEN CONCERNED, TO SAY THE LEAST, ABOUT THE POSSIBILITY OF RADIATION LEAKS. THIS FIASCO INSPIRED SEVERAL BOOK AND FILM TREATMENTS.

international

headlines

Chairman **mao tse-tung** launched the Cultural Revolution in China. Said Mr. Mao, "A revolution is not a dinner party, or writing an essay, or painting a picture, or doing embroidery; it cannot be so refined, so leisurely and gentle, so temperate, kind, courteous, restrained, and magnanimous. A revolution is an insurrection, an act of violence by which one class overthrows another." These words, from 1927, were being forcibly implemented to renew the revolutionary spirit of 1949. In China on August 1, the Great Proletarian Cultural Revolution picked up speed at the meeting of the Central Committee of the Chinese Communist party. The Red Guard, mostly teenaged revolutionaries, armed with their little red books, *Quotations of Chairman Mao,* published in Beijing, shouted slogans attacking "Soviet revisionism and U.S. imperialism."

In Dublin, in March 1966, the Nelson column, symbolizing British rule over Ireland, was bombed. The suspects were the outlawed Irish Republican Army.

War criminals Albert Speer and Baldur von Schirach left Spandau Prison after serving the 20-year sentences given them at **NUREMBERG.**

November in Florence: priceless artworks were destroyed by ravaging floods. Paintings, sculpture, and thousands of ancient books in the National Library were swept away or submerged. The Strozzi Palace and the Uffizi Gallery were hard hit.

Leonid Brezhnev became the top Soviet leader.

KWAME NKRUMAH OF GHANA FOUND HIMSELF DEPOSED DURING A MILITARY COUP BY HIS COUNTRY'S ARMY AND POLICE OFFICERS. HE WAS IN CHINA AT THE TIME.

'66

The Supreme Court narrowly ruled (5–4) a confession was invalid if the suspect was not informed of his rights in advance. **Ernesto Miranda**'s rape conviction was overturned. Now even the most law-abiding TV viewer knows the Miranda warning. Cops carry it on a palm-sized card even though they know it by heart and probably mumble it in their sleep: **"You have the right to remain silent....You have the right to an attorney...."**

THE POPULATION OF THE U.S. WAS 195,827,000.

AT SHEA STADIUM IN NEW YORK, 40,000 FANS SAW THE BEATLES PERFORM.

In New York, David Miller was convicted of burning his draft card.

truman capote had a spectacular year. His "nonfiction novel," *In Cold Blood,* about a murder spree in the heartland, was a literary sensation. Capote, credited with establishing a new literary genre, also was a society sensation. He hosted a famous Black and White Ball at the Plaza hotel, with publisher Kay Graham as guest of honor in her upswept harlequin eyemask and jeweled, fitted tunic. He was the hottest number on the social circuit, although diminutive, snippy, judgmental, and a gossip; the Tiny Terror, he was called.

cultural
milestones

MUHAMMAD ALI was reclassified 1-A by his draft board.

THE OLD METROPOLITAN OPERA HOUSE CLOSED IN NEW YORK AFTER 83 YEARS. **THE NEW MET,** DECORATED WITH MURALS BY MARC CHAGALL, OPENED AT LINCOLN CENTER.

VAN GOGH's portrait of Mlle. Ravoux sold at Christie's, London, for 150,000 guineas, which was then equivalent to $441,000 in the U.S.

television

There were an estimated 189,837,950 TV sets in the world, with the U.S. having the most, followed by Japan and the Soviet Union. There were 53,850,000 TV households in America, 93 percent. More than 5 million homes had color TV; 9.6% of TV households.

top-ranking tv shows of the 1966 fall season:

1. "Bonanza" (NBC)

2. "The Red Skelton Hour" (CBS)

3. "The Andy Griffith Hour" (CBS)

4. "The Lucy Show" (CBS)

5. "The Jackie Gleason Show" (CBS)

6. "Green Acres" (CBS)

7. "Daktari" (CBS)
   three-way tie with

   "Bewitched" (ABC) and

   "The Beverly Hillbillies" (CBS)

8. "Gomer Pyle, U.S.M.C." (CBS)
   four-way tie with

   "The Virginian" (NBC)

   "The Lawrence Welk Show" (ABC) and

   "The Ed Sullivan Show" (CBS)

"THE SMOTHERS BROTHERS COMEDY HOUR" (CBS) WAS #16 IN THE 1966–67 RATINGS. MOVIES ON TV, APPEARING SEVERAL YEARS AFTER THEIR THEATRICAL RELEASE, WERE VERY POPULAR. CBS OFFERED **"FRIDAY NIGHT MOVIES,"** TIED WITH **"HOGAN'S HEROES"** (CBS) FOR #17 IN THE RATINGS. **"SATURDAY NIGHT AT THE MOVIES"** ON NBC RANKED #20.

"batman" premiered on January 12 on ABC, one part of a long-lasting multimedia phenom in the world of superheroes. Live people make great cartoon characters, and sometimes vice versa.

LUCI BAINES JOHNSON, the President's daughter, married **PATRICK NUGENT** in a memorable Washington wedding. The marriage later ended in divorce.

milestones

celeb wedding of the year

FRANK SINATRA, 50, married **MIA FARROW,** 21, in Las Vegas on July 19.

SOPHIA LOREN and **CARLO PONTI** again tied the knot on April 9 in France. It looked slightly more legal the second time around, but Italian authorities still viewed Ponti as being married to his first wife. There was a complicated history of marriages, annulments, and divorces.

10

DEATHS

Lenny Bruce,
satiric genius and nightclub comic, often prosecuted on obscenity charges, posthumously immortalized in Albert Goldman's muckraking bio *Ladies and Gentlemen, Lenny Bruce!*, overdosed in August.

Hedda Hopper,
queen of the gossip columnists for 28 years, died at 75 on February 1, 1966.

Buster Keaton,
film actor and comedian best remembered for silent roles, died at 70.

Sophie Tucker,
the "last of the Red Hot Mammas," died at 79. She'd had a career of almost 60 years.

Montgomery Clift,
intense actor, died of a heart attack at 45. Best remembered for roles in *From Here to Eternity, Judgment at Nuremberg,* and *Freud.*

Other passages from the scene: **Walt Disney, Admiral Chester Nimitz, Lillian Smith** (author of *Strange Fruit*), American showman **Billy Rose,** comedian **Ed Wynn,** sculptors **Malvina Hoffman, Paul Manship,** and **William Zorach,** beauty titan **Elizabeth Arden,** and playwright **Russell Crouse.**

Lenny Bruce

births

MIKE TYSON, boxer, born June 30

CINDY CRAWFORD, supermodel married to Richard Gere, born February 20.

JANET JACKSON, actress/singer, born May 16.

JOHN CUSACK, actor, born June 26.

JUSTINE BATEMAN, actress, born February 19.

SINEAD O'CONNOR, sometimes bald singer, born December 8.

ALBERTO TOMBA, sexy Italian Olympian in skiing, born December 19.

11

'66

hit music

1. **i'm a believer** Monkees
2. **the ballad of the green berets** Sgt. Barry Sandler
3. **winchester cathedral** New Vaudeville Band
4. **(you're my) soul and inspiration** Righteous Brothers
5. **monday, monday** Mamas and the Papas
6. **we can work it out** Beatles
7. **summer in the city** Lovin' Spoonful

8. **cherish** Association
9. **you can't hurry love** Supremes
10. **wild thing** Troggs

other tunes that reached #1 on the pop charts

"Paint It Black" Rolling Stones

"Reach Out I'll Be There" Four Tops

"When a Man Loves a Woman"
Percy Sledge

"My Love" Petula Clark

"You Keep Me Hangin' On" Supremes

"Hanky Panky"
Tommy James and the Shondells

"The Sound of Silence"
Simon and Garfunkel

"Paperback Writer" Beatles

"Last Train to Clarksville"
Monkees

"Good Vibrations"
Beach Boys

"Strangers in the Night"
Frank Sinatra and the famous

**"These Boots Are Made
for Walkin',"**
by daughter Nancy Sinatra.

hey, hey, it's the monkees!

High-concept TV, a genuine cultural phenomenon exemplifying the youth culture, the nadir of Western civilization as we knew it, or just the crassest lowbrow commercialism of the decade? The Monkees were a totally manufactured, made-for-TV imitation rock group that homogenized both the mophead look and the rock 'n' roll sound in order to appeal to the younger set.

13

Jacqueline Susann

fiction

1. **valley of the dolls**
   jacqueline susann

2. **the adventurers**
   harold robbins

3. **the secret of santa vittoria**
   robert crichton

4. **capable of honor**
   allen drury

5. **the double image**
   helen macinnes

6. **the fixer**
   bernard malamud

7. **tell no man**
   adela rogers st. johns

8. **tai-pan**
   james clavell

9. **the embezzler**
   louis auchincloss

10. **all in the family**
    edwin o'connor
    *(no relation to the sitcom,
    nor to carroll o'connor)*

books

1. **how to avoid probate**
   norman f. dacey *(an unusual volume that offered advice on making wills and avoiding estate litigation and sold 575,000 copies)*

2. **human sexual response**
   william masters and virginia e. johnson

3. **in cold blood**
   truman capote

4. **games people play**
   eric berne, m.d.

5. **a thousand days**
   arthur schlesinger, jr.

6. **everything but money**
   sam levenson

7. **the random house dictionary**

8. **rush to judgment**
   mark lane

9. **the last battle**
   cornelius ryan

10. **phyllis diller's housekeeping hints**
    phyllis diller

ARTHUR SCHLESINGER, JR., WON HIS SECOND PULITZER, AS WELL AS THE NATIONAL BOOK AWARD, FOR *A THOUSAND DAYS.* KATHERINE ANNE PORTER ALSO WON BOTH LITERARY AWARDS, FOR HER *COLLECTED STORIES.*

Influential "Black Power" writers were widely read, in **The Autobiography of Malcolm X** and LeRoi Jones's **Home: Social Essays.**

THE BALTIMORE
ORIOLES BESTED
THE LOS ANGELES
DODGERS IN THE
**63RD WORLD
SERIES.**

**Casey Stengel and Ted
Williams were inducted into
the Baseball Hall of Fame.**

THE 70TH
BOSTON
MARATHON

was won by Japan's Kenji
Kimihara in 2 hrs., 17 min.,
11 sec. Roberta Gibb Bingay
was the first woman to run
in the event; she finished
ahead of about half the men.

**BILLIE JEAN KING BEAT BRAZIL'S
MARIA BUENO AT WIMBLEDON.**

Ted Williams

In football, the National and American leagues agreed to a merger to occur in 1970 and a common draft of college players in 1967. They also set up a plan for a **Super Bowl** game at the end of the 1966–67 season.

JACK NICKLAUS won the Masters golf tourney for the 3rd time. He won the British Open, becoming one of 4 to win the 4 major golfing events in the world (the PGA, the Masters, and the U.S. Open are the others).

IN PRO ACTION ON NOVEMBER 27, A NEW NFL SCORING RECORD WAS SET — THE HIGHEST COMBINED TOTAL POINTS IN A GAME AND THE SECOND HIGHEST FOR ONE TEAM : THE WASHINGTON REDSKINS BEAT THE NEW YORK GIANTS 72-41.

sports

bill russell, Celt center, succeeded Auerbach and became the first Black to coach a major American sports team.

PEGGY FLEMING WON THE WOMEN'S SINGLES TITLE IN FIGURE SKATING. SHE WOULD GO ON TO WIN 3 CONSECUTIVE WORLD TITLES.

THE BOSTON CELTICS prevailed in the NBA championships. They beat the Los Angeles Lakers 4 games to 3, and Red Auerbach, the Celtics' coach, retired with his 8th successive championship.

top box-office stars of 1966

1. Julie Andrews
2. Sean Connery
3. Elizabeth Taylor
4. Jack Lemmon
5. Richard Burton
6. Cary Grant
7. John Wayne
8. Doris Day
9. Paul Newman
10. Elvis Presley

HIGH–SALARIED **JULIE ANDREWS** MADE $125,000 FOR *MARY POPPINS* (1964) AND MADE $700,000 FOR *HAWAII* IN 1966.

ACADEMY AWARDS FOR 1966 FILMS

A Man for All Seasons won Best Picture Oscar, over *Alfie, The Sand Pebbles, Who's Afraid of Virginia Woolf?,* and *The Russians Are Coming, The Russians Are Coming.* **Fred Zinnemann** won Best Director for *A Man for All Seasons.* **Paul Scofield** took Best Actor honors, also for *Man for All Seasons.* **Elizabeth Taylor** won a well-deserved Best Actress Oscar for her role in *Virginia Woolf,* one of her most memorable performances. **Walter Matthau** was Best Supporting Actor for *The Fortune Cookie.* **Sandy Dennis,** who played George Segal's wife in *Woolf,* was named Best Supporting Actress. Best song was ***"Born Free,"*** from the film of the same name. Best Foreign Language Film was Claude Lelouch's ***A Man and a Woman.***

top money-making films

1. *Thunderball* ($39,000,000)

2. *Doctor Zhivago* ($15,000,000)

3. *Who's Afraid of Virginia Woolf?* ($10,300,000)

4. *That Darn Cat* ($9,200,000)

5. *The Russians Are Coming,
   The Russians Are Coming* ($7,750,000)

6. *Lt. Robin Crusoe, USN* ($7,500,000)

7. *The Silencers* ($7,000,000)

8. *Torn Curtain* (Hitchcock) ($7,000,000)

9. *Our Man Flint* ($6,500,000)

10. *A Patch of Blue* ($6,300,000)

NIPPING AT THE HEELS OF THE TOP 10 EARNERS WAS **THE UGLY DACHSHUND,** WHICH GROSSED $6 MILLION.

ALSO BIG: **WILD ANGELS, HARPER, THE BLUE MAX, FANTASTIC VOYAGE,** AND **THE GLASS BOTTOM BOAT.**

movies

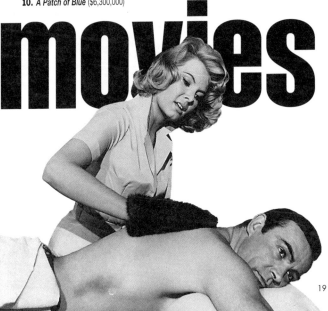

19

After 4 record-breaking years, production was down slightly, about 2.6%. Styling features were mostly along the lines of sporty "personal cars." Some of the new ones were the Mercury Cougar, Chevy Camaro, and Cadillac Eldorado. The Plymouth Barracuda was given a fastback.

cars

Ford Thunderbird added a four-door model. Dodge Charger, Ford Mustang, Buick Riviera, Olds Toronado, and Corvette were also popular choices. Styling concepts had European accents, such as the Italian-type wheel openings on the Plymouth Barracuda.

Congress held widely publicized hearings on auto safety, culminating in the Federal Traffic Safety Act. Carmakers announced that they'd introduce safety features in the 1967 models. Dual brakes and collapsible steering columns were among them. Ford featured shoulder harnesses for front-seat passengers.

Hemlines climbed to 5 inches above the knee for teens and young women (two to three years before, the norm had been midknee). In London, skirts 7 inches above the knee were noted. It was a great year for fashion, if you had great legs, or could artfully conceal their limitations in knee-high or thigh-high boots. The accent on legs was good for the hosiery industry; all manner of tights and stockings, in vibrant colors and textures, contributed to the Total Look. Shoes and boots, of course, also took on importance. The clunky heel and broad, round toe were prevalent. Although most footwear was "sturdy" looking, slingbacks were also popular.

It was *the* year of the mini.

fashion

ANDROGYNOUS FASHION. THE MOD LOOK.

LONDON, "SWINGING" LONDON, was the cradle of everything hip; *Time* declared it the city of the decade in April 1966. The Young English Look was influential. Carnaby Street was known around the world; one shop there had a sign: "Please excuse us if we call you Madam, Sir."

men in flowered shirts, wild ties, fancy footwear, and other peacock tendencies.

High-gloss makeup. Wet-look patent leather or plastic clothes. Silver dresses and raincoats. Paris proclaimed silver the color of the year in the fall showings—a space-age color.

It was a very good year for all shades of the color purple, from coolest mauve and lilac to the most intense plum. Goldenrod yellow, pale green, and Delft blue were also favored. Yet the military influence in clothing also brought out the importance of camel, navy, red, and white.

ACCESSORIES—**TINY LITTLE POUCHES** AND **SHOULDER BAGS WITH CHAINS. SAILOR CAPS, PARAMILITARY HATS,** OR **BERETS;** OTHERWISE NOT TOO MANY HATS SEEN ON FASHIONABLE HEADS.

final factoid

September 8, 1966 . . . "To seek out new life and civilizations. To boldly go where no man has gone before . . . " These were the missions of NBC's **"star trek."**

archive photos: inside front cover, pages 1, 2, 5, 6, 13, 21, 22, 23, inside back cover.

associated press: pages 3, 4, 7, 10, 11, 16.

photofest : pages 8, 9, 14, 18, 19, 25.

photo research:
alice albert

coordination:
rustyn birch

design:
carol bokuniewicz design
mutsumi hyuga

'66